KITSUNE

JANE McKIE

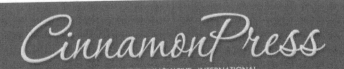
INDEPENDENT INNOVATIVE INTERNATIONAL

Published by Cinnamon Press
Meirion House
Tanygrisiau
Blaenau Ffestiniog
Gwynedd, LL41 3SU
www.cinnamonpress.com

The right of Jane McKie to be identified as author of this work has been asserted by her in accordance with the Copyright, Designs and Patent Act, 1988. Copyright © 2015 Jane McKie.
ISBN: 978-1-909077-84-3
British Library Cataloguing in Publication Data. A CIP record for this book can be obtained from the British Library.

Designed and typeset in Palatino by Cinnamon Press. Printed in Poland.
Cover design by Adam Craig from original artwork by Caroline List.
Cinnamon Press is represented in the UK by Inpress Ltd www.inpressbooks.co.uk and in Wales by the Welsh Books Council www.cllc.org.uk

Acknowledgements

I would like to thank the following publications, in which versions of some of the poems have appeared: *EarthLines* ('The Little Magisterium'), *Edinburgh Review* ('Every Town Creates Its Saint', 'Our Last Night in a Small French Hotel', 'The Specious Present', 'The Zephyr Aunts'), *The Dark Horse* ('Council Tractor Blocks the Road'), *Mslexia* ('Archipelago', which won third prize in the *Mslexia* International Poetry Competition 2011), and the *Journal of the Motherhood Initiative*, Volume 3, Number 2 ('Archipelago', 'Baba Yaga in the Grand Canyon', 'Burying My Mother's Library', 'The Monster of Ravenna's Mother'); '1976 Kodak', 'Cousteau Addresses Darwin at the Bottom of the Ocean', 'Garden of Bedsteads', 'Leper Window, St Mary the Virgin', 'Ostrich Egg Ex-voto', 'Rannoch', 'Scottish Voodoo', and 'Tentsmuir Point' all appeared in the 2011 Mariscat pamphlet, *Garden of Besteads*, and 'Leper Window' won first prize in the 2011 Edwin Morgan International Poetry Competition; 'The Boy Who Found Fear', 'I Almost Pronounce You', 'Lake above the Clouds' (with the title 'Mirrors in the Pyrenees'), and 'Sunrise over Lunan Bay' were shortlisted for the 2012 Manchester Poetry Prize; 'The Inland Lighthouse' was the result of an ASCUS micro-residency in association with the University of Strathclyde's Chamberlain Lab, which researches into the mechanisms and functional outcomes of S-acylation, a reversible modification that affects proteins, and is particularly important for neuronal function and plasticity; 'We Can't Escape the Fact That We're Not Enough for Each Other' was commissioned by the Talbot Rice Gallery as a response to Christopher Orr's painting, 'To Your Scattered Bodies Go'.

Thanks go to Jan and the dynamic Cinnamon team, to my dear 'wee group' (Patricia Ace, Anna Crowe, Vicki Feaver, Jillian Fenn, Steph Green, and Paula Jennings), to all the Shore Poets (especially Hamish Whyte and Diana Hendry for their warm Mariscat home), and to Peter and Ann Sansom and all the inspiring poets of the class of '12. Hearty thanks, as ever, go to Super-Phil, and also to the brilliant Davids – Messrs' Troupes and Wilson. Last but not least, thanks go to Caroline List for her witty and beautiful artwork.

Contents

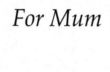

For Mum

Kitsune

Perhaps We Might Start Now

Perhaps we might be kind to each other
all the time (or, at least, as often as
we can). Perhaps we might propagate herbs,
creosote the fence, make sensory beds
for badgers and moles, for all half-blind beasts.

Perhaps we might begin assembling kit
for those trips promised to dark-sky preserves,
where we'll listen without interference,
camped together, tilting our heads to see
beyond the world's competing radiance.

Perhaps kindness is not simply action
but also foliation – benign buds
inside the brain preparing for their time
in wise, conciliatory silence.

The Inland Lighthouse

Her mind is opaque now, her moods impossible to read. Does she know
that, as Iris Murdoch put it, she's "sailing into the dark"?

Andrea Gillies, Keeper.

Nothing Makes Sense in Isolation

A neuron glowing under a microscope.
A single electric thought.

Its lassos of dendrites spread
lithe ropes into darkness

like a story laid out from beginning to end,
finished but not complete.

How Much Can the Patient Take?

They give you a ticket, tell you to go,
not on holiday, go

where bitter drinks
become milk;

where food strikes your tongue
and tangles with it;

where there are no stairs or stoves
and a body must accept softness.

They give you a ticket, tell you it's not
a cure. They give you a ticket

and you take it.

The Inland Lighthouse

Can a neuron outlive
the body that contains it?

Its blurt of fire
is arc lamp bright

but its dark
is as compelling –

the blue of every
in-between hour

laid side by side,
here and there,

signals less quick,
more sporadic.

There's no more need
of light –

lowlands abandoned
at the levee's break –

but it burns anyway,
can't seem to stop,

so when the beam
slides clockwise

and away, it draws
with it a comet-tail

of repeating glare
and shadow.

The Second Coming

2 a.m. In bed, she hears rain
break
like a flush across skin –

a thirst-quenching *shush*;
every golem under earth
stirs, waking to drink.

*

She presses kid gloves, lays them
in the drawer. They lend other fabrics
a whiff of department store. But the lacy
christening gown has richer history –
bought with coins saved up in a tin,
creased into quarters, counted as 'best'.

Of all the things she made or saved for,
this is the one that most resembles him.
When the drawer opens, up it rises,
fine white mist dancing over all the rest.

A Burning Woman

Mrs. Berry wears a tight topaz skirt
that everyone says is too young, too silky.
Her kid goes to a private school: my mum
wonders where the money comes from.

Mrs. Berry whispers to me at bedtime.
She says: *Carry the moth cupped in your palms
as if it is a flame* and *Take no notice of the rat
tugging at my veil* and *Leave us in peace.*

Every Town Creates Its Saint

This one has blonde Saint Susan,
the skin between her fingers so cracked
that people joked it would spread
into webbing, her speech so hushed
that people tired of listening closely.
As a toddler she was notably gentle,
her old-fashioned face turned always
to the sea. This continued for years
until she dropped out of college,
drove off in a Ford Cortina, friendless
mother to sand fleas, heading east
towards the cliffs and the cinematic
moment no one would witness.

Soon everyone observed her feast.

Ostrich Egg Ex-voto

I give you my egg,
not expecting you to be impressed.

What would you do with it, after all?

It is so big, so delicate,
a thought held in the head too long.

It was hung from a church beam in Athens,
phosphorescent in the dusk.

It was a sacred globe; now
it gathers dust on your Edinburgh shelf.

Nothing I do pleases you.

You're not to know a saint lives inside,
ticking like a foetus.

Garden of Bedsteads

They came from the German orphanage,
just frames, no padding, craving
the crease of hands around bars.

In the garden, they wept. Rust marks
on the grass stayed after they left,
after the lawn had been mown and mown.

"Remember the eggs," they pined.
"The dyed-red eggs at Easter time.
Under our pillows, painted with crosses –

the lightest of secrets.
Remember the walls that peeled to pink,
the ceiling that caved, plastering hair.

Remember the men who came with a van
and lifted us up from the gravel drive.
Already emptied. Corroding in air."

The Monster of Ravenna's Mother

My monster rides my hip. I think him perfect.

His one eye, a Caithness glass paperweight,
coddles a tiny empire of misfits at its heart,
clear euphony where only candles penetrate.

As for my heart, that's where a life of failure
curls, withered in scrutiny. But look at me
with my monster! The best thing I have made.

We Are All Wild Beasts

after 'Collioure' (1905) by André Derain

Collioure, straight from the artist's tube,
purged of any niceties, of toothless blues;
the sea's cast as Medea, as she always is,
tasting slightly of blood, as she always does.

Even in an empty gallery, far from crowning light,
the sea spreads her legs. No one polite around,
no studied oglers. Just the sun-
baked roofs with slopes like parched tongues.

Loving the Last Wild Pig

Such a bristling beast,
contour is his signature –

the bulbous wattle folded
at his throat, the berries

of snot around his snout –
but he's as fragile as anyone.

Hair of fire-cured tobacco,
a moustache of snuff,

when he runs, his knees
scream *Meeeeeeeee*

and the ground remembers him:
the plum of him, the thistle.

He never registers sky,
his rheumy eyeglasses

are always down. The loose
skin on his haunches is leather

(as it has been since the womb).
Loving him won't be easy,

but think of the ugly umbilicus
that once filtered your own waste

and know you will come to
resemble him, as surprised

by your saddle of flesh
as you are by the lessening

of effort. There will be pities.
There will be delicacies.

The Grove

You come into the grove carrying jugs
of Breton cider. They smell of rivers,
of junket, of rot, of overblown flowers,
their abundance lapping bright as lava.
We empty every one. This ritual drink
to ease our affair fills us with visions
of antlers and tusks, a forest of musk.

When it is over we lie side by side
to stare up at sky between the branches,
our story pooling in our hollows, slick
with waning portent, wanting to be sung.
But we hesitate, not even talking.
Trees grow above us, gigantic, swollen,
while we shrink into our separate bones.

Kitsune

I dip my fingers in the rills
of your sleeping body,
bluish where the moon
brushes them, and notice

my nails need filing.
In this moment of peace
I can grow into a fox again –
tricksy, whiskered,

intoxicating – forgetful
of how, with a mirror
and razor, I will make
myself into a veil or shell;

I will lather and scrape
at my skin, taking it back
to the skin of a girl, because
it is my mask you love.

A Feral Child Inside

To have been unschooled,

left muddy and befouled
in a forest; to feel flakes

of snow on lashes without
being able to say 'snow';

to have an insatiable taste
for uncooked meat, flavours

locked; to hear only creaks
and whistles, never music;

to have no home, to never
have had a home; to be part

of a fairytale, to not know
the story –

this is the story.

Baba Yaga in the Grand Canyon

The Cariboo Road

They keep coming, the empty-handed, with just one more shrew-
sized question, its answer unravelling another year of Baba Yaga's life.

They leave their hunger on the snow of her skin.

She is a wise woman; surely she can boil up another brew of roses,
those bitter lilac cabbages, to sift in the hot swill of her samovar?

Her own medicine. The answer is clear.
Leave this place. Don't grieve forever.

                    *

From New Westminster to Yale,
from Yale to Quesnel:
after Alaska, this is a rush of gold,
a skein of wheel-ruts and waterways,
trail of melded nights and days
that never once feels wearisome.

Her palms itch with preludes.

Baba Yaga Confesses to the Colorado River

Stifled in her size zero fleece, hidebound
by magic, Baba Yaga goat-steps
the theatre of umbers
down to the distant basin.

After kicking off her walking boots,
she stands where the Colorado River is shallow,
candle-flamed by brack and flicker,
thinking back until she cannot bear to think.

                    *

The river says:

Swap your birch for Chihuahua pines.

Look, here are trees with fat buttery berries,
a redcurrant sun roasts the Grand Canyon's skull.

Grandmother, forget your cupboard love
of captured children, give up your keyhole

of icicle teeth, the bone staves
encircling your chicken-legged hut.

Stop under these generous cliffs;
let them eat you with their light.

She says: I have grown up.
I have grown old.

She says: I have nurtured.
I have murdered.

The river says: Let go of the orphan stones in your pocket.
Unlace your spine. Follow me. Where I go

there are no contradictions.

The Compassionate Thief

Pink pebbles in the river's gullet
give Baba Yaga as much pleasure
as children stolen from their beds.

She sieves them, non-committal
prospector, tips them back in.
Sieves them, tips them back in.

*

A late summer storm approaches.
She welcomes the cast of the sky
as it shifts again, thunderclouds
scaled in CinemaScope.

Secreted between shelves
of rock and more rock: blue lupine
and Indian paintbrush. Wild turkeys.
Tarantulas on the high flats.

All the horizontals make her dizzy.
When summer lightning hits,
her feet run from the river's forgiveness,
propelled by spidery rhythms.

The Motherless Province

At night, a hundred questions flock,
settling in nearby trees to hector
in a Slavic tongue she can no longer
make sense of.

She shifts her fitful tatters of sleep,
trying to believe in the soft motel bed.

*

Come, wake up the children.

A wolf hangs his head, digs in the compact
snow for frozen crumbs of blood. Another
has his neck in a yoke, ready to serve,
but there is no mistress, no alpha beast
to measure himself against. Trees are milk
on one side, coal on the other. The moon,
on the cusp, holds up the old world order,
presides over a stopgap parliament.

Between the trees, a chaos of boulders
are flint-faced crouching men. All empty-ones
gather, wait with the rocks for their mother.
When the moon sets, she will surely return.

Burying My Mother's Library

Patricia Cornwell, Aleksandr Solzhenitsyn,
Mrs. Molesworth's *The Cuckoo Clock*.

The modest pulp of them mattresses larvae,
helps a pathologist pinpoint time of death.

You show me a body bag that doesn't leak.
And they are always hungry. And always shoeless.

And wet. Year after year they build their nests
and hatch their eggs; year after year, I suppose,

the old ones gradually die off, and the young ones
take their place. Under earth, books hatch words.

They elongate into sentences, squirming
to be pieced together.

The Underground Observatory

I watch things flourish:

pale rhizomes and spores,
white vermicelli nematodes,

excreta, burgundy with berries.
There is so much succulence,

rooty treasure-troves big
as dragon bones, half a boot,

bread that is no longer bread,
cobwebbed apples, rusted lids.

At the ragged feet of walls
groundwater collects

in pockets between soil,
black as chewed tobacco.

I want to catch them all,
these gripes and shifts:

stone without the power
to rise and stone that heaves

haphazardly, the slow mill
of landfill, the threadbare

weave of my once-best suit.

Leper Window, St Mary the Virgin

The contagion of lepers
has lifted.

The low glass, where they crouched
even lower,

remains, but their breath,
their rash, their lack,

has passed into the lace
of shadows in the yard.

Where God looked
but did not touch,

the lip of sandstone
is purled with fissures.

Viking Horse-bone Ice Skates

The horse won't know how its metatarsal
can be whittled by friction with the lake,
how the act of skating is part halting
glide, part planer blade; or how thick ice melts
back to health, its grooves, its scuffed 'v's, softening
to fill their own wounds. And the horse won't know
how the skating boy, who opens his mouth
as he flies, will lose three blunt teeth, two milk,
one new; how these teeth, also, will be found.

Encounter in the Ice Hotel

Dwarfed in the cavernous lobby,
we are vibrating at the frequency

of turquoise, our soft palates throb
with the pain of being clean.

Even the mundane process of checking-in
elicits a surprising clarity.

I wish for a candelabrum of tears,
an operatic prop.

You wish for an orthopedic bed
to take the edge off your sciatica.

A surprise in the night – me,
beside you again, under furs.

In the morning, I am a sealed
carton of clothes; you, a folded note.

The Ocean Describes Montauk Point

I cast stones at it,
calling it a harlot.

I want it, only to lose my hunger.
Resent it, only to drown my anger.

I travel its complexities, its runes,
carving them into more civilised forms.

I second-guess my motives,
and the untranslatable, otiose

drunken vows I murmur.
I have no intention of grand amour,

yet I welcome its love, fearing
my indifference; I relish its nearness

then run a mile. I worry we behave
like parent and child, man and wife;

worry
that's all there is to our story.

Lake above the Clouds

I

The placenta of a lamb.
I almost step in it. The smell of the caul
catches, something long-dead
but still shining.

II

Griffon vultures. They wheel, send an image
of embers to the backs of my eyes.

III

A cloud of butterflies,
wings freckled with peppercorns.
They staple themselves to my hands and face
to feed off the salt.

IV

A stand of irises, starling blue,
laid out on the slope. Dressed simply
for a mountain funeral.

V

Iron crosses at intervals along the pass.
I kneel because kneeling
is better than walking by.

VI

A slab of rock like an altar.
It shelters buds I can't identify,
pink stalks and low gluey leaves
like hands extended softly.

VII

A woman walking in the opposite direction,
red hair, the voice of a chough.
She tells me jokes in French.
I realise I haven't spoken
for over a week. "My husband is behind,"
she says. "Typical man."
I continue but don't meet anyone.

VIII

My wristwatch. Time falls from it
in black ellipses.

IX

A tiny lake dwarfed by pinnacles,
the Ibón d'Ansabère, according to my map.
From a distance an emerald drop of ocean
lodged miles above sea level.
As I stride down and into it
the cold burns, warns me that liquid
can solidify. It mimics then inverts the sky.

X

The reflection of my body in the lake,
distorted.

XI

The sun
as it crawls out of smallness, intensity.
It readies itself.

XII

Descending cloud, without taste
or warmth. It looks like smoke, drifts
over, rubbing out every shape.

XIII

The pine trees a smudged line of kohl.
I make for their shelter.

XIV

The moon, never the same twice,
like this memory.
The stars ferocious, even in summer.

The Wind in the Mountains

Fulfillment lies in leaving:
wind on the empty pool.

This easterly is a shadow remade.
It lifts the shallows of your skin

unkindly, a bit of a bully,
brings an early freeze

no amount of wine will thaw.
Dinner on the terrace and in by ten,

fretting over boutique hotels
at the right intervals along the route—

They will spring up from anxiety
and buckle as soon as you depart.

Only the act of leaving will endure.
The wind in the mountains knows it.

Our Last Night in a Small French Hotel

Before dawn I saw bones of birds
in the pendant shade; as first light
laid épées across the floor,
I spied shed feathers in your clothes.

I woke again when mid-morning
brought rain to my nostrils.
Windows wide, the air blue,
a high altitude silence to our room.

We Can't Escape the Fact That We're Not Enough for Each Other

Brambling, bullfinch, chaffinch, crossbill,
goldfinch, greenfinch, hawfinch, redpoll –

a new edge between us scissors
through air, routing music
        from throats, birds from perches.

They spill, forming
flurries like snow but
        tough as flint

and I feel every atom of
their shifting,
        flickering wingbeats.

Nightjar, nuthatch, dipper, pipit,
woodlark, shorelark, skylark, swallow –

I had birds once.

        I let them go.

The Ringing Sky

In the middle of our move, Nan says she hears the house
talking for the first time, its voice like a wineglass chime,
ringing behind us, diminishing as we drive down the
street with the first load. It is like that to live with her.
Her hunches. Her sayings. We smile and seldom
contradict even the most extravagant of statements. She
rules us as a small god might a pocket universe—

The sky
when we lift it

prickles with newness, a new bulge
in skin that is a deeper hue than we remember

as if it had been mislaid, or left in a corner
to be forgotten.

And now we come to move it for her
(because we have to move everything)

we see all its colours differently, nod
to one another when its shape

resists containment, knowing
the crates she orders are strong.

Culs-de-sac

I have so much to learn –
that violets are more blue than pink,
that lawns can smell of mine shafts
after rain, that a new home
can take a lifetime to inhabit.

The flowers in their peat moss beds
look lost; when a Boeing's four engines
thrum overhead, petals quake under
a sharklike shadow that's smaller
than the noise. Am I wrong to object

to these violets with their after-burn
of slate, their flimsy assertions
of place? They are not the wild,
dogged bulbs I have buried in
my body. Nevertheless, they grow.

Archipelago

My husband levitates at night: birds begin
to vibrate, snow sifts from the curtains,
and I wake to see him lift an inch, cat-curled
on his side, soft as bread. He faces away
but I can tell he smiles, every breath huffs
upwards. I don't touch him. I fear his rest,
worry my stranger's reach will stop his heart.

My mother searches drawers at night: thunk
thunk – I know they're empty, the next room
made hollow with the slap of resinless MDF,
its peculiar Calvinism. What does she look for?
Not folded vests, broderie anglaise, not scalloped
necks or figure-hugging skirts; she prefers
pantsuits these days, the shed skins of shapes.

My daughter lines her tired eyes at night: violet
or ultramarine, even when she stays at home.
I can hear the tinny iPod dreaming, its tsking
irks me like no other sound – insectoid,
subtly overbearing. At least she's here.
It makes me wince, finding a vein in my head,
but it tsk tsk tsks my melancholy girl to sleep.

My son is like my husband at night: lost
to the pillow without complications.
The book he reads behind his lids might shock me.
I choose not to enquire – of myself, or of friends
with famished boys. It is enough to know
his hair smells like pan-drops, his lovely feet
slop over the bed. He is an open lotus flower.

The Little Magisterium

*That preparation which alchemists believed would convert any baser
metal into silver.*

My daughter calls it The Blue Tomorrow,
at her bedroom window just before dawn
when our garden has the cast of moonlit snow.

I look towards our back fence and see slow
frost-melt, saliva of ice on the small hawthorn.
My daughter calls it The Blue Tomorrow.

I examine her averted face. I don't suppose
she's awake, she's pale as a goat's horn.
Our garden has the cast of moonlit snow.

Our two reflections in the window throw
shapes like half-formed beasts across the lawn.
My daughter calls it The Blue Tomorrow.

I want to become her, know all she knows,
just for a moment, before the silver's torn
and our garden has the cast of moonlit snow

and nothing more. Silly really, what's below
has been there since before she was born.
My daughter calls it The Blue Tomorrow
when our garden has the cast of moonlit snow.

Midsummer

Greenswarm
(unknown phylum)

flit between branches,
blur of sun and metal.

When they settle, singing,
snapping, they turn

to art deco clips
worn to an al fresco party.

The smell of aspen,
and the last atoms

of the perfume of the last girl
to leave – *Vetiver* by Guerlain –

accompany their flight.
At the edge of the glade

is a white silk blouse
blessed with the ache

of the nearness of grass,
impression of skin, veined

bulb-lilac-green, drenched
with the taste of crow garlic.

They've Had Their Time

There needs to be a divestment:

the embryos of chalk horses, schema
curled into the turf of hills; the Mays,

those polyester and sequin girls,
their sensitive scalps, their diesel-fumed floats;

the end-of-school balls, repetitive,
circling like midges—

All seeds destined for paper
packets and pale maturation.

*

Rusky wasps have laid their galls
to redden into oak apples.

Inside one, autumn parts her lips.

Council Tractor Blocks the Road

There is a spray of grass from the giant mower
trundling ahead at twenty miles an hour.

The confetti of August on my windscreen, blades
green, blades sere. A joyous exhalation and a massacre.

Winter Bread

Our mouths know no other bread.
Chestnuts every meal, sawdust and sweetness.

The gaps between Ma's calls grow longer
as I grow taller, losing myself in the thickets,

fighting with pigs. Strong as a boar whose tusks
score the ground, I use finger bones.

In the daily rummage for spiny cases,
pigs nick my arm, wallop my ribs;

I bite them back and taste the butter
of chestnuts under hoary old skins.

They howl, eyes pink. I know they fear me:
their haunches tremble like empty flour sacks.

I am the pig with a girl for its ghost,
the one who can wrestle twenty glossy hulls

from the pockets of their cheeks.
But I love those stupid fierce-snouts

as I love my starving brothers.

Scottish Voodoo

Winter fruit rest on a vine suspended
from a metal gate, weight black against snow.
Strung by their feet they make a grisly sight –
rack of Norway rats, a farmer's warning.
Frozen totems to mutilate our walk.

They are so stark we have to blink, shake flakes
from our eyes, focussing the monochrome.
We notice the folds of ears, the wear of
teeth. Not theirs, ours. There is the tannic taste
of someone's private rancour in our mouths.

Rannoch

A wilderness peopled by ifrits:

The first a hinny, horse-headed-mule-legged, running
with a sideways gait
against the wind. She brays.   Stops.
                      Brays.   Stops.
Her teeth are the yellow first light on a lochan.

The second an orange-eyed rowan, small berries
the quickbane of an autumn coupling.
Birds peck them to jam before seeding
                                    mountains.

The third a fire, thatch of russet grasses.
They gutter the whole year.

The last black cinders, cooling.

Tentsmuir Point

Somewhere in the dunes
we hear a man's voice,
There is time aplenty.

Such an old-fashioned phrase,
so out of place above the screech of bathers
taking breaks from the waves.

Time for what?
For the lawn.
For that novel.
For having kids.

We want to hear more
but the wind's up
whiting our ears with its playful skirl.

*

The culverts and ramparts
   trip us –
sand-rimed chevaux de frise –
and I think about defences,
the land's soft buffers
bunching against invading seas.

How many scarps and counterscarps are in sight?
Their hundred blonde heads are bowed, intent on making trenches
to wait in, to watch from.

*

Look at that comber!

Long as a giant nemertine
squalling its body to shore.

We are safe from the worm, sheltered
by sackcloth and ashes.

*

We find calligraphy
collapsed
into Aramaic.

It might have been a name or two,
one scored under the other
with a foraged stick,
Kevin and Nuala
or *Lorna and Sean*
or *Colin and Emma*.

More than a weather vane,
its arms are many and they radiate.
It is a wind-rose
picking out the paths of couples like us
who have stumbled here
only to end up frozen.

*

Years later, climbing the bluff
is hard-going,
boots sinking into its side.
When I reach its saddle
my toes are lagged with sand.

I gaze at the teemless desert,
cloud-hued on an overcast day,
haven only to flickering wicks of marram.

It warms me, this nothing.

I Almost Pronounce You

His face a full pink cloud.
Her face a fawn's thin skull.

Under crow-whipped blossoms –
trees cherrying the pool
with confetti – long drinks
sit bottoming their souls,
dysphoric Kir Royales.

The marquee's stressed fabric
puckers behind their backs.

Nothing must tear today.

Straggles of relatives
are ushered across lawns
to witness a union
so gravid with tension
only the guy-ropes sing.

Easy Breakfast Muffins

Awake, O north wind; and come, thou south; blow upon my garden, that the spices thereof may flow out. Let my beloved come into his garden, and eat his precious fruits.

Song of Solomon 4:16

It's nippy out; I have to button my cardigan after I set the tray down
where you crouch, sprinkling turmeric to deter ants, abandoned
coffee cooling. I sniff at wisps of it. All flavour is in its vapour.

Here's your muffin, I say, and you half turn, mumbling your thanks.
It's fresh, I think, and new: a recipe for Easy Breakfast Muffins.
Sugar, raisins, cinnamon. The fragrance of Lebanon.

I was warm in the kitchen, captivated; now I am cold and free.
Eat, I want to shout. Eat. Before I throw dregs at your abstraction.
Before I leave you to your ants, to your brickdust-orange cordon.

The Zephyr Aunts

There is an orchard where breezes
are aunts.
They fill the space between trees
with womanly scents,
offer themselves as chaperones
on this, the warmest day of the year.

Take them up on their offer –
they will be watchful
while fanning themselves. Zelda,
the one with the witch's name,
will sniff at a russet until she declares it
"totally unfit for human consumption."

Marianne will ship her acquired
Spanish manners to the picnic,
clapping repeatedly at any zesty
remark, a dash of Catalonia
on the air – orange
and strong mountain fennel.

And Connie, who loved her husband
so fiercely, will be the first
to jump on the idea of marriage
when you test it aloud.
No timid chastisements
as you might expect of a zephyr,

but branches tormented –
a mini-cyclone around you,
picnic disrupted, memories
overturned. Ridiculous:
as if the world has room
for only one good marriage!

All three will sniff at your intended,
buffet the vigorous apple tree
you use to prop your back –
far too common, all fissured bark.
They fuss as you unscrew
another ripe globe from a branch.

This may not be what you want –
draughts at your wrist to freshen
your doubt. But they will be right.
You are too young. Before they died,
they knew enough between them
to live peaceably in the garden.

Honeymoon at Matlock Bath

Chinese dragon, galleon, gondola –
they shine on the Derwent like a comet
parading its tail beside Lover's Walks.

We wolf down chips, soak up the sulphurous fumes
of fireworks and motorbikes, our skins stewed
in illuminations: horse and carriage;

steam train; swan. They pulse, febrile and corny.
For one night only, we are pyretic –
more than 'you' and 'me' – like hamadryads

igniting a path through September trees.

Les Marais Mouillés

The marshes are molten bottle, moss ink –
a slowed down, thick algal oar-stroke.
                              Colour
is almost a dimension. Even chinks
of sky are chlorophyll-stained, and poplars,
latticed by light and leaf-print, start to glow
like skin does during croup.
                              (I remember
fighting a childhood fever, hot rosehips
drawn to my cheeks, my four year-old temper
soothed only by indolence and shadow.)

This is a good place to flatten the blood,
to forget the photosensitive world,
healing instead in one screened under mud,
duckweed. A bird hide. A diffuse green gut.

Cousteau Addresses Darwin at the Bottom of the Ocean

Your desk
has slipped underwater;

indigo ink spots spread to mirror
the skin of bluefaced angelfish,

wood marbles with longing
like all submerged things.

Desk legs, like mine, look bandy this deep
but are firmly tabled in sand,

open drawers contain
a school of snappers.

Here, one sees things differently,
without the close scrutiny

of peers: a cup coral
is the Holy Grail,

the flower of the mangrove
an opera glove

abandoned on the tide.
With my aqualung, I propel myself

to unprecedented depths.
I see creatures not unlike us.

An eel rests his grey cheek
against the solace of leather

seeking words to describe
his otherworldly hunger.

You do the same, your notebook
half-eaten, encrusted with a blush

of minute and tender animals.
Above us, my *Calypso* calls.

Gift from Queenie, May She Rest in Peace

She gave me a box of bath salts like uncut emeralds
pulverised to powder – greyish-blue and gritty.
I put them, with the clementine from my stocking,
at the bottom of my list of favourite gifts,
and forgot them. Only now, years later, do I run
them under water, worry they are so ancient
they will stain my skin. Worse – lace the heat
with arsenic green, leak an Aztec hex into the suds,
turning me as mean as their giver. I soak for hours
until I look as old as her, like wrinkled fruit;
until I see her face in mine and feel my heart contract.

Mesmerism

Not rich rich. Rich as a pensioner
who owns her own flat, rich as the
rare chance to enjoy a laugh.

Her true wealth, the wealth she values,
is a glass vase of a blue so spellbinding
it deserves a better name than *blue*.

"Indigo," she says, drawing it out – "In-di-go."
Plain glass, but in delicious thrall
to buried ice, to imperial Persia.

A streak of midnight on the mantel,
it warps her face into a fairground pitchman's –
acquisitive, all deep lines and nose –

until she *is* the pitchman,
a blackguard rolling bills between his palms,
never far from his reflection.

The Boy Who Found Fear

Boy made of sand
carries a black swan underarm
to jimmy windows, lift
all those little rubies
that wink in the small hours like digital clocks.
And as he crosses thresholds, lintels,
the grains of him unpick steadily
through the night,
ticking minutes, seconds
till he's caught.

The man and his wife
get home. There he is –
black feathers on the floor,
pile of sand so powder-white
it makes them recall their Gold
Coast honeymoon and weep.
The thieving boy! They sweep him up
into a pan, chuck him out.
He can't speak to tell them: *Stop,
I'm sorry.* A real boy at last.

Sunrise over Lunan Bay

The audible clink inside a bulb
as it ceases to fire.
Glass egg. It's always a performance,
a morning like this, opals in the east
and then a swarm of rain.

I eat a wet baguette on the beach.
Last night's wine dies in me,
last night's watered-down talk.
The sun struggles to get up. I applaud
the effort. My knuckles are raw

from forgetting to pack gloves.
When I have ideas they always stall like this –
with an apology, an audible clink
above the waves, something small
ceasing to fire.

The Specious Present

The short duration of which we are immediately and
incessantly sensible.

William James

He'll never get to Myrtle Farm today,
he thinks. He woke up with the bloody shakes.

Not today, he thinks. The duvet's calling
as prickly and cloying as a thicket,
clock hands tremble on the same damn minute,
while trees overhanging the stable roof
dangle burly limbs to drop in a storm
and he can't begin to lift the chainsaw.

Tomorrow, he thinks. He'll drive Long Furlong
willing the milometer to whizz round
those miles to where the A27
nuzzles the Downs and white slip roads lead to
Myrtle Farm and Myrtle Farm lies in state
like a lovely embalmed Eva Perón.

Empire of Sundaes

Swallow your coke-float:
drowned swans of cream, subsiding

bergs, long-handled spoon
to herd lumps into nullity.

The tall glass is planed,
glacial, sweating beads.

Sweet, corrosively sweet,
this urge to live in the past,

to guzzle a fizz of days
spent in a shallow pool

that lingers on the palate
more potent than the days themselves.

Eat me. Drink me.
I am delicious ice.

1976 Kodak

One.

The light,
opaque, shines from the left,
opening up the beach
into a silver dinner plate.

Two.

It is dark,
blues are an aquarium,
a cathode ray screen on a dull day.

Three.

Mum finds us.
Jim has the thermos.
His long torso is so white and spare
it reminds me of Christ on the cross;
he has the same pained air,
eyes always downcast.
The background is shiny toecaps.

Four.

All the gloss
seems to have rubbed off.
There is a stippled patch that tacks
to fingertips like terry-towelling
or sloth. Lorna buries herself in sand.

Five.

In the final picture, Mum got it right –
we are all huddled, perfectly centred, flax-headed
thistles elbowing each other (off camera),
smiling our barbarous milk teeth.

The Infernal Garden

I wander the chalk garden
trying not to cry.

Lost in my blue jumper
knitted with wormy wool –

too warm for Sussex in the '70s.
I knew my way once,

but bushes have sprung up
along the path, its brickwork

spiralling towards gaping carp,
those ageless, pig-lipped brutes.

I have to shade my eyes:
childhood is migraine,

white, anarchic;
it is a chalk wall

hollowed out of hillside
that makes the perfect screen

on which to read
the disappearing sky.